PragerU is redefining how people think about media and education. Watched millions of times every day, PragerU is the world's leading nonprofit with educational, entertaining, pro-American videos for every age. From intellectual, fact-based 5-Minute Videos and powerful personal storytelling to animated shows made just for kids—PragerU helps people of all ages think and live better.

PragerU Kids teaches history, civics, financial literacy, and American values to children across the K-12th grade spectrum. With kids shows, books, and educational resources for every grade, PragerU Kids offers content that parents and teachers trust and children love. Watch for free and learn more at PragerUkids.com.

Published by PragerU

15021 Ventura Boulevard #552

Sherman Oaks, CA 91403

Kerri Strug

Sometime around 1981, a four-year-old girl in Tucson, Arizona sat in awe. She was watching her older sister Lisa attending gymnastics class. The four-year-old, named Kerri, saw Lisa gracefully perform acrobatic moves, flipping and twisting through the air with ease. As she watched and admired her sister, Kerri felt the urge to see if she could do the moves herself.

Soon, Kerri was imitating Lisa, doing cartwheels and handsprings all over their house. It wasn't long before Kerri was hooked. She loved gymnastics, and she wanted to do it all the time.

It was then that Kerri's journey into the world of competitive gymnastics began. What she didn't know was that the next fourteen years of her life would be filled with both glorious victories and crushing setbacks. By the time her gymnastics career was over, she wasn't just an Olympic gold medalist—she was a legend who had inspired millions of people around the world.

GETTY IMAGES

FUN FACTS:

⭐ During her career, she was listed at four-foot-eight-inches tall.

⭐ Like other sports legends, she has appeared on the cover of the Wheaties cereal box.

⭐ She loves eating pizza and her favorite chewing gum brand is Bazooka Joe.

⭐ Since retiring from gymnastics, she continues to stay active by running marathons.

⭐ She is a big basketball fan and roots for the Arizona Wildcats, the UCLA Bruins, the Phoenix Suns, and the Houston Rockets.

⭐ She has appeared on several TV shows, such as *Saturday Night Live*, *The Today Show*, *Beverly Hills 90210*, and *Touched by an Angel*.

"I learned once and for all that no matter how much you try to prepare for every conceivable possibility in your life, there are always unexpected surprises."

Childhood

Kerri was born to a Jewish family on November 19, 1977 in the desert city of Tucson, Arizona. Her father, Burt, was a doctor who specialized in heart surgery. Back in high school, Burt was very active, playing baseball, tennis, and football. While Kerri inherited her father's athleticism and work ethic, she inherited her mom's gracefulness. Her mother, Melanie, raised Kerri and her siblings, Lisa and Kevin, but in her free time, she practiced ballet. Dance was her mother's lifelong passion.

Kerri was a shy girl—so shy that she was terrified of talking with other kids. Gymnastics, however, gave her confidence. She later asserted,

"I was born to do this sport... nothing and no one was going to stop me from trying."

Early Career

Although her sister Lisa eventually quit gymnastics, Kerri stuck with it. She began participating in meets around Arizona. In one of her earliest meets, she finished first in her age group. She was so advanced, she skipped two levels of competition.

Soon, Kerri was traveling across the country and the world to perform. She was very busy, not just because of gymnastics but also with her schoolwork. Despite the heavy load, she did well in the gym and the classroom, winning meets and getting straight A's.

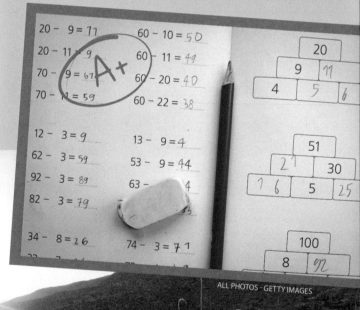

ALL PHOTOS - GETTY IMAGES

GYMNASTICS

Gymnastics is a sport where athletes perform acrobatic feats, such as flips, handstands, jumps, and turns. For every move, judges determine the gymnast's score, usually based on how hard the move was and how well the move was executed (which is scored out of 10 points).

Three Types of Gymnastics

Rhythmic:

A form of gymnastics emphasizing dance-like rhythmic routines, accentuated by the use of clubs, balls, ribbons, or hoops.

Artistic:

The best-known type of gymnastics, which usually involves demonstrating both power and precision.

Trampoline:

The newest form of gymnastics, which involves jumping and tumbling in the air.

Skills

Handspring:

A skill in gymnastics where you spring your body backwards or forwards off of your hands.

Giant:

A skill where you swing all the way around the high bar with your body stretched out in a straight position.

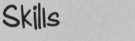

Double Back:

A skill you do on the floor where you flip twice before landing.

Yurchenko:

A skill on the vault that involves putting your hands on the vault sideways, like a cartwheel, then flipping backwards off the vault onto your feet to land.

Artistic Gymnastics Events

Vault:

An event in which gymnasts run down the runway, take off from a spring board onto a table-like object, perform handsprings, flips, and twists in the air, and then land on their feet on the floor.

Floor Exercise:

An event in which gymnasts perform routines that include dances, jumps, and tumbling passes on a roughly 40x40 foot square floor.

Beam:

An event in which gymnasts balance and perform exercises on a narrow, 4-inch horizontal bar made of wood, metal, and suede, raised off the floor.

Bars:

An event in which gymnasts use a cylindrical fiberglass bar held about five (low bar) to eight feet (high bar) above the floor to swing and execute flips and twists. The bars are often set at different heights for the gymnast, which together are called "uneven bars."

All-Around:

A category of gymnastics that includes all of the events. The person who earns the highest score from all the events combined is the winner.

Kerri's Dream

By 1990, Kerri was twelve years old, and she had a bold dream: to compete in the 1992 Olympics that would be held in Barcelona. It was a daunting challenge—going to the Olympics meant competing against the greatest athletes in the world, but she was determined to succeed. She moved to Texas to train with Béla Károlyi and his wife, Martha. She practiced hard but also found time to take up hobbies and have fun outside of gymnastics. She watched movies, read books, practiced painting and pottery, and talked regularly with her family. Kerry later wrote,

"I would advise any elite athlete... get a life outside of your athletic world."

THE LIFE OF A GYMNAST

Kerri's training in the Károlyis' program consumed almost her entire life. This is what her average day looked like, six or seven days a week (times are approximate):

Sunrise-10:00am

Conditioning:
Floor jumps
Sit-ups (hundreds)
Pull-ups

Practice Gymnastics Routines:
Vault
Floor Exercise
Beam
Bar

10:30am-2:30pm
Attend school

3:00pm-4:00pm
Naptime

4:30pm-End the Afternoon
Physical Therapy (needed to rest the body)

Start of Evening until 9:00pm/10:00pm
Practice for optional routines and learning new skills.
Private lessons on specific skills,
routines, or choreography (as needed).

Road to Barcelona

The process to qualify as an Olympic gymnast is very rigorous, full of endless training and competitions, where one must perform well in one meet to qualify for the next.

To get selected for the 1992 Olympics, Kerri participated in several events starting in 1991 and did very well. The final test was in June of 1992, at the Olympic Trials in Baltimore. There, she finished in third place out of 12 total people, which qualified her for the U.S. Olympic team. At the age of 14, she was the youngest American to compete in the Barcelona Olympics. She wrote in her diary,

"I've accomplished a dream... I've got to call Mom and Dad with the great news."

The 1992 Olympics

Kerri was at the highest level of gymnastics in the world, but the pressure only got more intense. During the Olympics, she did well on the bars, with a score of 9.862, and the vault, with a 9.95. Her performance helped the team win a bronze medal, which officially made her an Olympic medalist. It was a great accomplishment for a 14-year-old.

The thrill of winning the medal, however, turned into crushing disappointment when she found that, in her individual score, she finished just behind her teammate Kim Zmeskal by a miniscule .014 points. That meant that she wouldn't make the all-around competition. After years of hard work, Kerri's Olympic experience was over. For Kerri, it was all an emotional rollercoaster. She wrote in her diary,

"It's really weird. I got an Olympic medal and I'm miserable."

GETTY IMAGES

More Heartbreak

Kerri's disappointment fueled her determination to come back even stronger. She wanted to compete in the 1996 Olympics in Atlanta.

Achieving that dream, however, would be a lot harder than she imagined.

First, during a competition in Stuttgart, Germany, she had a bad fall while on the beam and suffered a severe tear in her stomach muscle. Kerri would be out for six months.

After recovering, she competed in an event in Palm Springs, California. During the meet, she had yet another nasty fall while doing bars—this one resulting in a stress fracture in her back. Again, she was out for months, this time suffering from fainting spells and severe back spasms.

Suffering two major injuries back to back left Kerri so discouraged that she even considered quitting. Frustrated, she told her dad,

"I'm cursed!"

Kerri also had her share of insecurities. She still struggled with shyness and there were other more famous gymnasts. Sometimes, she felt people overlooked or ignored her and focused on her competitors. As difficult as these insecurities were, she refused to quit. Instead, she used them as motivation to become better.

BOTH IMAGES – GETTY IMAGES

GETTY IMAGES

Road to Atlanta

By 1994, she had recovered and felt refreshed and confident. She competed around the world with the other great U.S. female gymnasts, like Shannon Miller, Dominique Moceanu, Amanda Borden, and Dominique Dawes. They all pushed each other to be the best they could be.

Kerri was performing better than ever before. Béla even remarked, "I see something happening. This fragile-looking kid is lion-hearted."

At the Olympic Trials in June 1996, she finished second place out of 13 competitors, which secured her a spot on the U.S. Olympic team. Kerri was now a two-time Olympian. It was a great accomplishment, but the job wasn't finished: she wanted a gold medal.

"I wanted Atlanta. Nothing and no one was going to keep me from reaching my dream."

The 1996 Olympics

Shannon, the two Dominiques, and Amanda joined Kerri on the team, along with Amy Chow and Jaycie Phelps. No U.S. Olympic team had ever won the gold before in the women's team competition, and they wanted to be the first. Although they had spent years competing against each other, this time they truly came together as a team. They had seen each other overcome injuries and disappointments and now felt more like friends rather than rivals.

In the first events, Kerri performed well on the floor, earning a 9.825, and the vault, with a 9.812. The team as a whole found themselves barely trailing Russia for first place. That night, Kerri wrote in her diary,

"We're all ready. We're going for the gold... Go USA!"

"I was eighteen. But in terms of gymnastics, I was a hardened, experienced veteran... Nothing on the gymnastics floor scared me anymore."

The next day, there were 32,000 fans, including Kerri's parents, packed in the Georgia Dome to watch the team finals. As the competition began, the team performed well on the beams and the floor. They just had to make sure not to fall during the vault, and the gold would be theirs.

Things, however, didn't go as planned. Shannon scored a 9.7 and a 9.662 on her vaults, which was lower than expected. The spectators and the millions of Americans watching on TV feared that the gold was slipping away.

Then, Dominique Moceanu went up for her vault. The crowd gasped in disbelief as she fell on her first AND her second vaults, earning just a 9.2. Meanwhile, the Russian team was performing well and getting strong scores. Team USA's gold medal dreams seemed to be slipping out of reach.

GETTY IMAGES

Kerri's Moment (July 23, 1996)

All eyes turned to Kerri. As she ran and took off, her first vault "felt perfect," and she flipped and twisted through the air in a move called the Yurchenko 1 1/2. Then something went wrong: she landed sooner than she thought she would and fell backwards. The crowd gasped again. She was stunned and embarrassed, since she rarely fell in previous competitions.

Even worse, she felt a "pain... like none I had ever had before" in her ankle. Kerri knew something didn't feel right and wondered if she should still try her second vault. She believed, however, that the gold was at stake.

The whole world watched as Kerri lined up again for her second vault. For millions of viewers, there was no way Team USA could win the gold with another fall. America's hopes seemed to rest on Kerri's shoulders.

Kerri quietly said a prayer to herself, "Please, God, help me out here." She began to run, later writing,

> "It felt like my ankle was swinging loosely from the rest of my leg."

She lept, then flipped and twisted through the air. Unlike previously, she had enough distance from the ground to pull her legs under her to land. She landed perfectly, and then heard a rip—the sound of the tendons in her ankle tearing even further.

Somehow, she found the strength to hold a finishing pose—a pose that confirmed for the judges she had completed her vault. This time, as she landed, she did not fall.

GETTY IMAGES

11

The crowd went wild, including Kerri's parents. Millions of people watching on TV cheered as well. As the pain in her ankle spread across her whole leg, Kerri collapsed onto the mat. She could no longer stand.

Kerri had done it. She scored a 9.712. Team USA had won the gold. Kerri couldn't believe it and was in a daze as the crowd chanted "USA, USA!" Since she couldn't stand on her own, Béla carried Kerri up to the staging area for the medal ceremony. When the national anthem was played, Kerri got emotional. She had finally achieved her biggest dream, and she thought to herself, "You've been waiting for this all your life. Thank you, God." Then, Kerri and all her teammates received their gold medals. The joy of victory was enough for her—for a moment—to forget about the intense throbbing in her leg.

"One strange, unexpected moment in Atlanta proved that just when you believe your dreams have been shattered, everything can come together and you're vaulted into a world where dreams come true."

GETTY IMAGES

"You've been waiting for this all your life. Thank you, God."

National Hero

Even though there were more gymnastics competitions remaining in the Olympics, Kerri was done. She had a severe **lateral sprain** on her ankle and could no longer compete. But it didn't matter. She had attained her goal as a newly-minted gold medalist and become a national hero.

Later on, people noticed that Team USA would still have won the gold without Kerri's second vault. They knew this by looking at the final scores the Russians got when it was all over. When Kerri was lining up for her second vault, however, that wasn't clear because the Russian gymnasts hadn't completed their events and gotten their scores yet. Kerri did her second vault believing that the pressure of a gold medal was on her shoulders and she had succeeded.

Kerri's success was even more remarkable because few expected her to be the hero. Many sports writers focused more on her teammates, such as Shannon Miller and Dominique Moceanu, while ignoring Kerri.

In a sense, she was an underdog. There is no doubt that the team won the gold together. In the end, however, it was Kerri who gave the world a truly unforgettable moment.

"The very time we spent competing with one another drew us closer... We had fallen down a thousand times, but we always got back up."

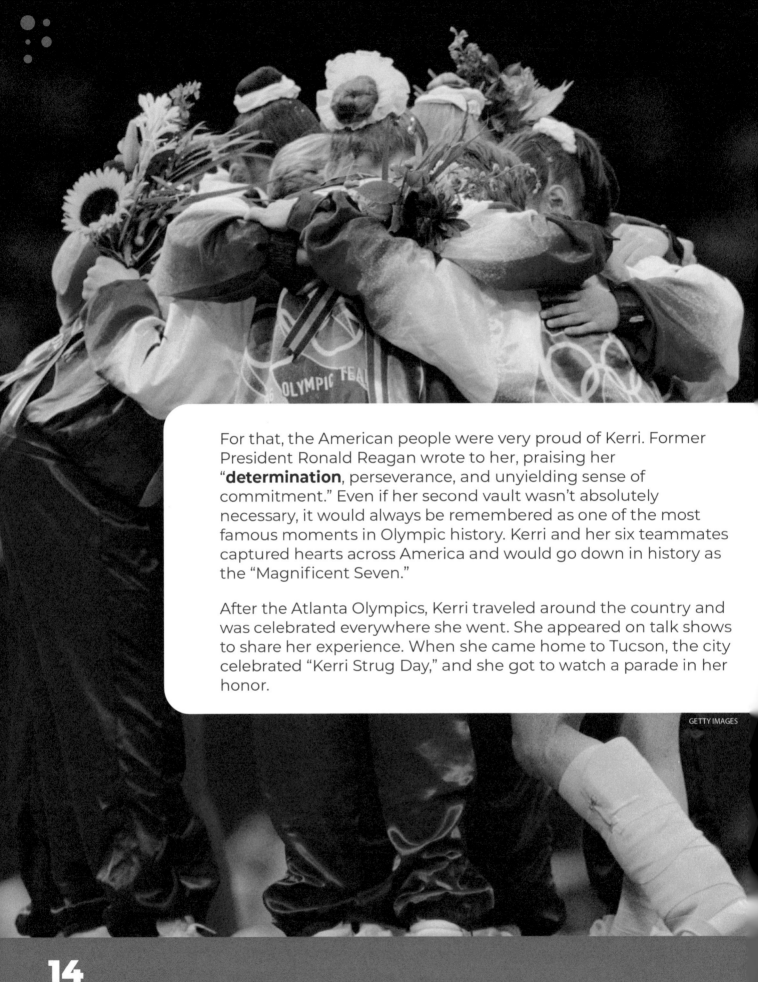

For that, the American people were very proud of Kerri. Former President Ronald Reagan wrote to her, praising her "**determination**, perseverance, and unyielding sense of commitment." Even if her second vault wasn't absolutely necessary, it would always be remembered as one of the most famous moments in Olympic history. Kerri and her six teammates captured hearts across America and would go down in history as the "Magnificent Seven."

After the Atlanta Olympics, Kerri traveled around the country and was celebrated everywhere she went. She appeared on talk shows to share her experience. When she came home to Tucson, the city celebrated "Kerri Strug Day," and she got to watch a parade in her honor.

GETTY IMAGES

After Gymnastics

After achieving her dream in Atlanta and after all of the celebrations, Kerri's Olympic days were over. It was time to move on to the next stage of her life. She decided to attend the University of California, Los Angeles. She later transferred to Stanford University, graduating with master's degrees in communications and social psychology.

Kerri has moved on from gymnastics and has been living a pretty ordinary, happy life. In 2010, she became Kerri Strug Fischer after marrying a lawyer named Robert Fischer. They now have two children. For millions of people around the world, however, she will always be a legend and an inspiration—as the **resilient** 18-year-old girl who overcame pain and heartache to win her country the gold.

Kerri at the White House after the 1996 Olympics

GETTY IMAGES

A LIFE OF SERVICE

Ever since the 1996 Olympics, Kerri has lived her life serving others in many ways. After graduating, she taught children at Tom Matsumoto Elementary School in San Jose, California.

Not many people know that Kerri also got involved in public service. In 2003, she moved to Washington, D.C. and worked for President George W. Bush's administration. During her time in the administration, she worked, first at the White House, then at the U.S. Department of Treasury, and finally, at the U.S. Department of Justice. Even though she was well-known, she quietly worked hard, focusing more on serving others than drawing attention to herself.

GETTY IMAGES

PHILANTHROPY

Kerri has spent many years working with various organizations that help people in need:

Cal Ripken, Sr. Foundation: Helps build character and teaches life lessons to disadvantaged young people.

Child and Family Network Centers: Provides high-quality, free education services to at-risk children and families.

Gene Spotlight: Supports research to find treatments and cures for rare genetic disorders.

ING's Run For Something Better: Supports youth running and fitness education in schools.

Junior League of Washington: Encourages volunteerism, developing the potential of women, and improving communities.

Main Street Theater: Promotes a lifelong appreciation of theater among young people.

March of Dimes: Works to prevent birth defects, premature birth, and infant mortality.

Prader-Willi Syndrome Association: Serves people with Prader-Willi Syndrome and their families.

"I can't explain the thrill I always have felt when I'm flying through the air, spinning and turning, performing at my very best. When I hit the mat, plant my feet, raise my chin, and throw out my hands in the finishing pose, it's the greatest adrenaline rush in the world."

PERSONAL BEST:

Sports legends are made by trying to beat their own best scores. They practice every day.

Try this fitness challenge today and again in two weeks after daily practice. How much did you improve?

Today:
In one minute

In Two Weeks:
In one minute

Sit-ups:_____   Sit-ups:_____

Push-ups:_____   Push-ups:_____

Jumping Jacks: _____   Jumping Jacks: _____

THE PHYSICS OF GYMNASTICS

Being a gymnast means using physics to manipulate your body in extraordinary ways. A gymnast often takes advantage of **gravity**, which is a **force** that pulls us all towards the ground, and **torque**, a force that causes something to rotate. For instance, when you are swinging around on a bar and on your way down, gravity pulls you down, which causes you to accelerate and generate **momentum** to continue swinging back up.

Performing vaults are difficult, especially because you have to land perfectly and remain standing. There are many different forces acting on your body that you have to control when you land. All of those forces end up centering on just one part of your body—your feet. In fact, the forces one experiences upon landing are similar to the kinds you feel when you are on a rollercoaster. Imagine jumping off a rollercoaster on its way down and trying to land on the ground without falling!

WHAT CAN YOU LEARN FROM KERRI STRUG?

Vocabulary

Stress Fracture: A small crack in a bone.

Fainting Spell: When you lose consciousness for a short period of time, often because your blood isn't getting enough oxygen.

Spasm: A sudden, involuntary movement.

Lateral Sprain: An injury where ligaments, which connect muscles, in the ankle are stretched or torn.

Determination: A characteristic where a person never gives up no matter what kinds of challenges they face.

Resilient: Able to bounce back from a difficult situation.

Gravity: A force that attracts objects towards one other.

Force: An influence (a push or pull) on an object that can change its motion.

Torque: A force on an object that causes it to rotate.

Momentum: The amount of motion occurring in an object that is moving, calculated by multiplying the object's mass with its velocity.

GOLDEN ATTRIBUTES:

Being a gold medal champion takes hard work and determination. List as many other attributes you learned from Kerri as you can:

PICTURE YOURSELF AS A CHAMPION!

Use the space provided to draw a portrait of yourself and your favorite sport. One day you could become a sports legend yourself! Send your cover to kidsbooks@prageru.com for a chance to be featured on social media!

SPORTS Legends BIOGRAPHIES:

OLYMPIANS

KERRI STRUG

ERIC LIDDELL

LINOY ASHRAM

HERB BROOKS

KERRI STRUG

COLLECT ALL THE OLYMPIAN TOKENS!

Cut out and paste tokens for each of the the 4 featured Olympians onto the spaces above.

Sources

"Biography." *Kerri Strug: Official Web Site of Olympic Gold Medal Gymnast*,
https://www.kerristrug.info/biography/. Accessed 25 August 2022.

Berkow, Ira. "GYMNASTICS; After Vault, Strug Finds Balance in Life." *The New York
Times*, 8 November 1997,
https://www.nytimes.com/1997/11/08/sports/gymnastics-after-vault-
strug-finds-balance-in-life.html/. Accessed 25 August 2022.

Cooperman, Rachel. "Where Are They Now: Kerri Strug." *ESPN*, 27 June 2012,
https://www.espn.com/olympics/summer/2012/espnw/story/_/id/8103144/kerri-stru
g/. Accessed 26 August 2022.

"Glossary of Terms." *USA Gymnastics*,
https://usagym.org/pages/gymnastics101/glossary.html/. Accessed 28 August 2022.

"KERRI STRUG." *USA Gymnastics*,
https://usagym.org/pages/athletes/archivedbios/s/kstrug.pdf/. Accessed 25 August
2022.

La Duca, Patty. "With Kerri Strug." *The New York Times*, 27 September 2008,
https://www.nytimes.com/2008/09/28/sports/olympics/28seconds.html/. Accessed
25 August 2022.

Penner, Mike. "The Day After." *Los Angeles Times*, 25 July 1996,
https://www.latimes.com/archives/la-xpm-1996-07-25-ss-27813-story.html/.
Accessed 25 August 2022.

Strug, Kerri and John P. Lopez. *Landing on My Feet: A Diary of Dreams.* Andrews
McMeel Publishing, 1997.

GETTY IMAGES

We're reaching America's youth with PragerU Kids!

With kids shows, books, and educational resources that teach classic American values, PragerU Kids offers content that parents and teachers trust and children love. As a nonprofit, PragerU relies on the generosity of donors committed to helping us spread messages of liberty, economic freedom, and Judeo-Christian values to the next generation. PragerU Kids is the leading network with educational, entertaining, pro-American content for every grade. Watch for free and learn more at:

PragerUkids.com

25618550R00017